Let's Get Healthy

Your Food

Sarah Ridley

W
FRANKLIN WATTS
LONDON • SYDNEY

This edition first published in 2008 by Franklin Wat[ ]

Franklin Watts
338 Euston Road
London
NW1 3BH

Franklin Watts Australia
Level 17/207 Kent Street
Sydney NSW 2000

Copyright © Franklin Watts 2004 and 2008

Let's Get Healthy is a reduced text version of *Look After Yourself!*
The original texts were by Claire Llewellyn.

Series editor: Sarah Peutrill
Art director: Jonathan Hair
Design: Kirstie Billingham
Illustrations: James Evans
Photographs: Ray Moller unless otherwise acknowledged
Picture research: Diana Morris
Series consultant: Lynn Huggins-Cooper

Dewey number: 613.2

ISBN: 978 0 7496 8320 7

Printed in China

Acknowledgments:
Professor N. Russell/Science Photo Library: 18cr
Sinclair Stammers/Science Photo Library: 24t

With thanks to our models: Emilia, Holly, Jerome, Lewis, Mandalena and Wilf.

Franklin Watts is a division of Hachette Children's Books, an Hachette Livre
UK company.
www.hachettelivre.co.uk

Let's Get Healthy

Your Food

Contents

Food, food, food!

There are so many kinds of food. How do we know what to choose?

What shall I eat?

Food is all around us. It is even sold at the swimming pool.

I ate too much!

Good for the body

Your body needs food to grow, and to stay fit and healthy.

Different foods help us in different ways.

These foods give us energy.

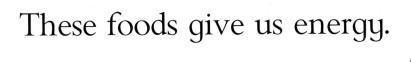

These help us grow.

These give us energy
and warmth.

These help us
stay well.

Choose
a mixture
of foods.

All kinds of food

You need to eat lots of different foods to stay healthy, not just your favourite food.

No foods are bad for you, but sugary foods harm your teeth.

Most of us like sweet foods, but they make our teeth decay.

A healthy start

When you wake in
the morning, your body
needs food and drink.

Wake up!

Toast

Orange
juice

Cereal

Egg

Fruit

Bagel

Croissant

Breakfast helps you get up and go. It helps you be active.

Don't skip breakfast!

Keeping going

By the end of the morning, you begin to feel hungry. Time for some lunch!

My tummy is rumbling!

This is a healthy lunch.

The last meal of the day gives us energy until bedtime. It allows our bodies to work all night long.

Bananas are a healthy snack.

Check the date

The date on food packages and cans tells you when to throw them away.

Unopened, these last for years!

5 years

2 years

2 years

3 years

3 years

Some food lasts for a month or more in a freezer.

Fresh foods don't last long.

2 days

4 days

1 day

BEST BEFORE

14 SEP

The 'best-before' date tells you how long the food will last.

Germs spoil food

Where are the germs?

Tiny things called germs are everywhere.

On the cat...

and on you!

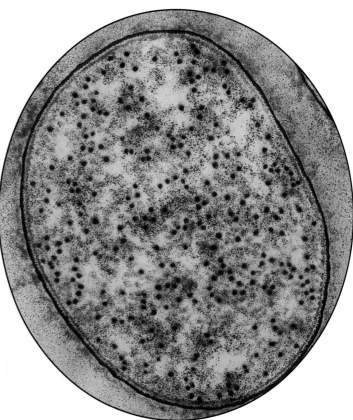

A magnified germ

18

Germs spoil fresh food and make it go bad.

Mouldy cheese

Sour milk

Bad food smells nasty!

Rotten tomatoes

Keep food cool

Fresh foods need to be kept in the fridge. The cold helps to stop germs from spoiling them.

The fridge will not keep food fresh forever.

Throw away food before it goes past its 'best before' date.

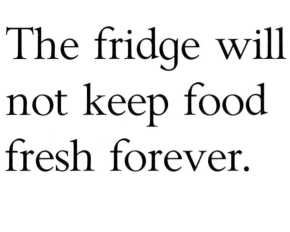

Keep it clean

Always wash your hands with soap and water before you touch food.

Keep the kitchen clean.

Always wash fresh vegetables, fruit and salad.

Remember that germs are invisible.

Getting ready to eat

Keep food covered, or in the fridge, until you are ready to eat it.

Flies spread germs!

Cats and dogs carry germs. Don't let them touch your food.

Feed pets away from your food.

25

Eating together

It's fun to share food with family or friends.

Supper's ready!

At the end of the meal, it's time to wash up. Leave everything clean for next time.

Everything is clean.

Glossary

active   To be moving, working and doing things.

best-before date   The date on food packaging that tells you how long the food will remain safe to eat.

energy   The power we get from food, which lets us work, grow and keep warm.

fresh   Fresh food has been made or picked recently. It is not stale, dried, canned or frozen.

frozen   When something is so cold it turns hard. Frozen food can be stored for a long time.

germs Tiny living things that can spread disease.

healthy Fit and well.

magnified Made to look bigger.

mouldy Mould is green or black fungi that can grow on food and spoil it.

sour Food with a sharp, nasty taste. Milk turns sour if it is left in a warm place.

to spoil To go bad. Spoiled food is mouldy or stale and should not be eaten.

sugar Something that is found in many foods and makes them taste sweet.

Index

About this book

Learning the principles of how to keep healthy and clean is one of life's most important skills. **Let's Get Healthy** is a series aimed at young children who are just beginning to develop these skills. **Your Food** looks at how to have a healthy diet and teaches simple food safety rules. To encourage a positive relationship with food it does not dwell on so-called 'unhealthy' foods, but stresses a balanced diet. For older children the book could be used as a starting point to explore other food safety issues, for example, using equipment such as knives correctly and cooking food.

Here are a few suggestions for activities children could try:

Pages 6-7 Discuss the range of places where food can be bought – supermarkets, local shops, markets, farmers' markets etc.

Pages 8-9 If appropriate, introduce the correct terms for the four food groups – carbohydrates, proteins, vitamins and minerals and fats. Children could write food diaries for a week and work out which group each food belongs to. They could then decide whether they have had a balanced diet.

Pages 10-11 Do a class or group survey of favourite foods and present the results in a bar chart.

Pages 12-13 Investigate what people eat for breakfast around the world by writing to pen-pals or relatives abroad.

Pages 14-15 Discuss favourite snack foods. Which ones help children 'keep going' longer?

Pages 16-17 Collect together packaging from various different types of food and then try to find the best-before dates.

Pages 18-19 Write 'a day in the life of a germ' story. The germ may be living on a dog, then get transferred to a hand when someone strokes the dog, and so on.

Pages 20-21 Draw stick people and decide what they might say about keeping food in the fridge.

Pages 22-27 Make a fruit salad, using these pages as a guide.

This Little Tiger book belongs to:

_____

_____

_____

More fabulous books from Little Tiger!

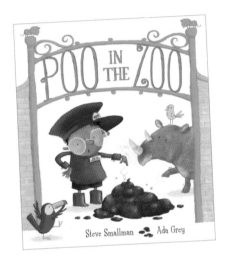

POO in the ZOO

Steve Smallman & Ada Grey

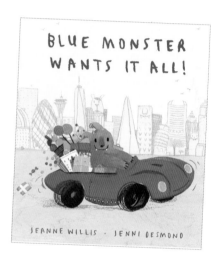

BLUE MONSTER WANTS IT ALL!

JEANNE WILLIS • JENNI DESMOND

CoCk-a-dOoDle-POO!

Steve Smallman • Florence Weiser

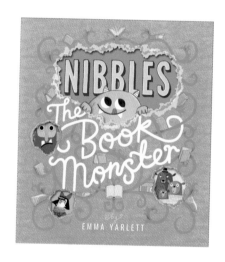

NIBBLES The BOOK Monster

EMMA YARLETT

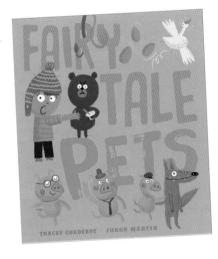

FAIRY TALE PETS

TRACEY CORDEROY • JORGE MARTIN

CAN I JOIN YOUR CLUB?

John Kelly • Steph Laberis

LITTLE TIGER

For information regarding any of the above books or for our catalogue, please contact us: Little Tiger Press Ltd, 1 Coda Studios, 189 Munster Road, London SW6 6AW
Tel: 020 7385 6333 • E-mail: contact@littletiger.co.uk • www.littletiger.co.uk

For Marion x ~ A R

For Nicole and David x x x ~ HG

LITTLE TIGER PRESS LTD,
an imprint of the Little Tiger Group
1 Coda Studios,
189 Munster Road,
London SW6 6AW
Imported into the EEA by
Penguin Random House Ireland,
Morrison Chambers, 32 Nassau Street,
Dublin D02 YH68
www.littletiger.co.uk

First published in Great Britain 2012
This edition published 2018
Text copyright © Alison Ritchie 2012
Illustrations copyright © Hannah George 2012
Alison Ritchie and Hannah George have asserted their rights
to be identified as the author and illustrator of this work
under the Copyright, Designs and Patents Act, 1988
A CIP catalogue record for this book
is available from the British Library
All rights reserved

CD contains:
1 - complete story with original music and sound effects
2 - story with page turn pings to encourage learner readers to join in

Running time over 15 mins
Music composed by Christopher Sarantis
Story read by Anna Crace
This recording copyright © Little Tiger Press Ltd 2018
℗ Christopher Sarantis

ISBN 978-1-78881-031-9
LTP/2700/4361/1121
Printed in China
10 9 8 7 6

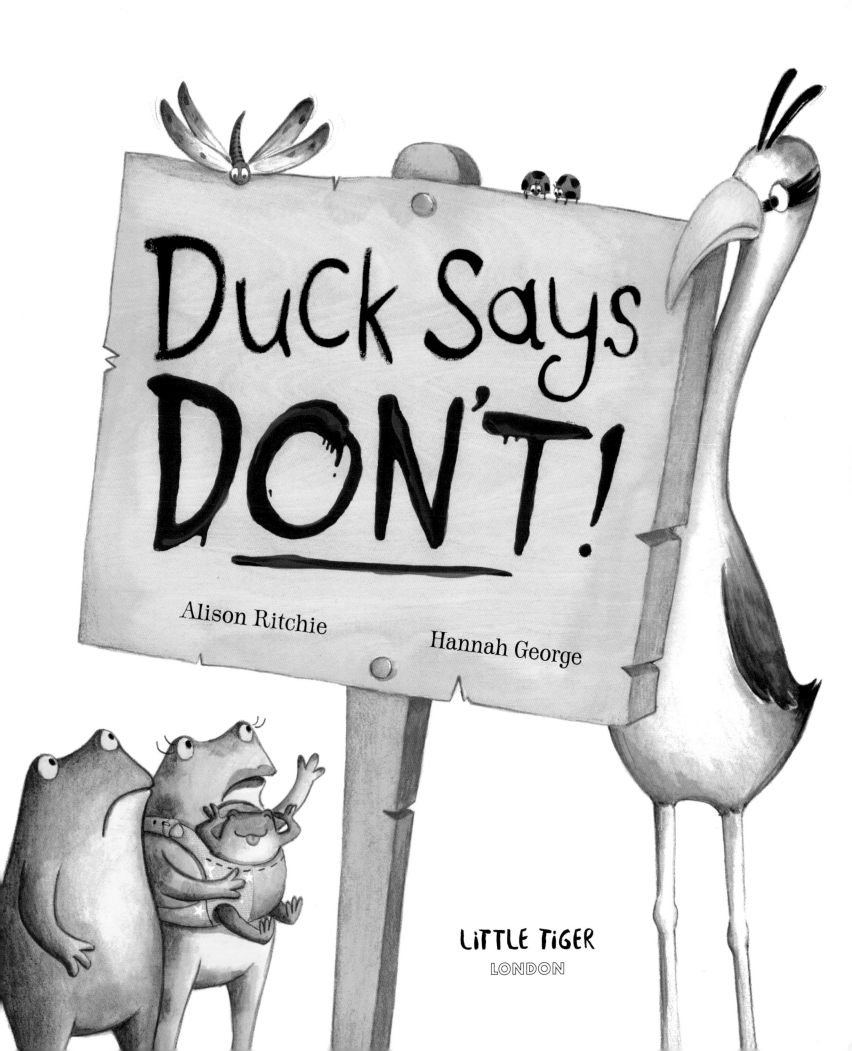

Duck Says DON'T!

Alison Ritchie

Hannah George

Little Tiger
LONDON

Duck lived on Goose's pond.
It was a **beautiful** pond. The water
was clear and sparkly, the sun shone
and everyone was **happy**.

One day, Goose told Duck, "I have a **very** important job for you. I am going on holiday, and I want **you** to look after the pond while I'm away."

Duck could **not** believe it.

"Goose wants me to look after the pond," he thought. "I am in charge!"

"Goose, I will do my very best," he promised.

The next day, Duck was up early watching over
his beautiful pond. Suddenly he spotted
the dragonflies racing.

"Stop that!" he quacked.
"I am in charge of this pond, and
you should **not** be buzzing
about all over it!"

FINISH LINE

"We're flying, Duck," said the dragonflies
in surprise. "That's what we do!"
   "Not here you don't,"
said Duck.

"That's told them,"
he thought. But just to
make sure, Duck fetched
some wood, and hammered
late into the night...

The next morning there was a sign in the pond.

Later that day, Duck saw Kingfisher fishing.
"Hey!" he shouted. "Stop that!
Fishing is not allowed here."

"Then where can I fish?"
said Kingfisher sadly.
"Somewhere else!" snapped Duck,
and he waddled off with his bottom in the air.

He fetched more wood and got busy
with another sign.

Duck was just having a little nap when the frogs dived into the water,

SPLASH!

"Frogs!" Duck yelled.
"What do you think you're doing?
Diving is forbidden!"

"Forbidden?"
said the frogs angrily. "Says who?"
"Says me," snapped Duck. "Duck!
Duck in charge of the pond!
So get out right now!"

Duck sat down happily. "Peace at last!" he thought.
But he couldn't settle. He looked at his perfect pond.
The sun was shining, the air was still
and there was
not a splash, buzz or
plop to be heard.

In fact there was **nothing** to be heard. It was **much** too quiet!

"**Where is everyone?**" wailed Duck. "What have I done?" He jumped up in a panic and flew off to find his friends.

NO FISHING
DUCK'S RULE (must be obeyed)

RACING!
der of Duck
(in charge of pond)

As Duck reached the meadow, he saw them playing together.

"This is fun," buzzed the dragonflies. "No bossy Duck telling us off!" croaked the frogs.

A tear fell down Duck's cheek. With a heavy heart he turned around and waddled back to Goose's pond.

The friends were snoozing in the afternoon sun
when they heard hammering coming from the pond.
"Can you believe it?" muttered the frogs.
"That duck is putting up MORE signs!"

The banging went on deep into the night.
Next morning there was an ENORMOUS
sign in the meadow…

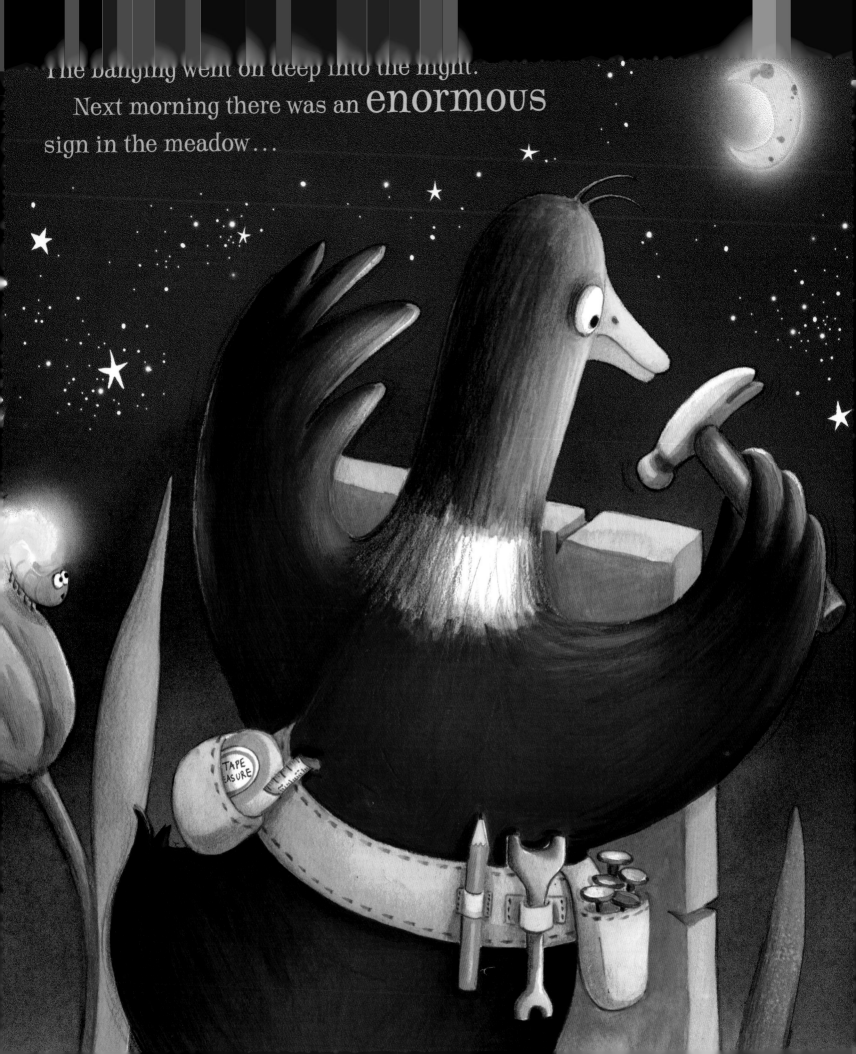

Duck is Very, Very SORRY!

PLEASE COME BACK.

This message is for the dragonflies, frogs and kingfisher,

from Duck xx

When the friends arrived at Goose's pond, they saw other signs too:

"Silly Duck!"
chirped Kingfisher.
"We've missed you!"
"Even though you were **very** bossy,"
chuckled the frogs.

When Goose came back from holiday,
she said, "Duck, you've done a **grand job**!
I'll leave you in charge next time."

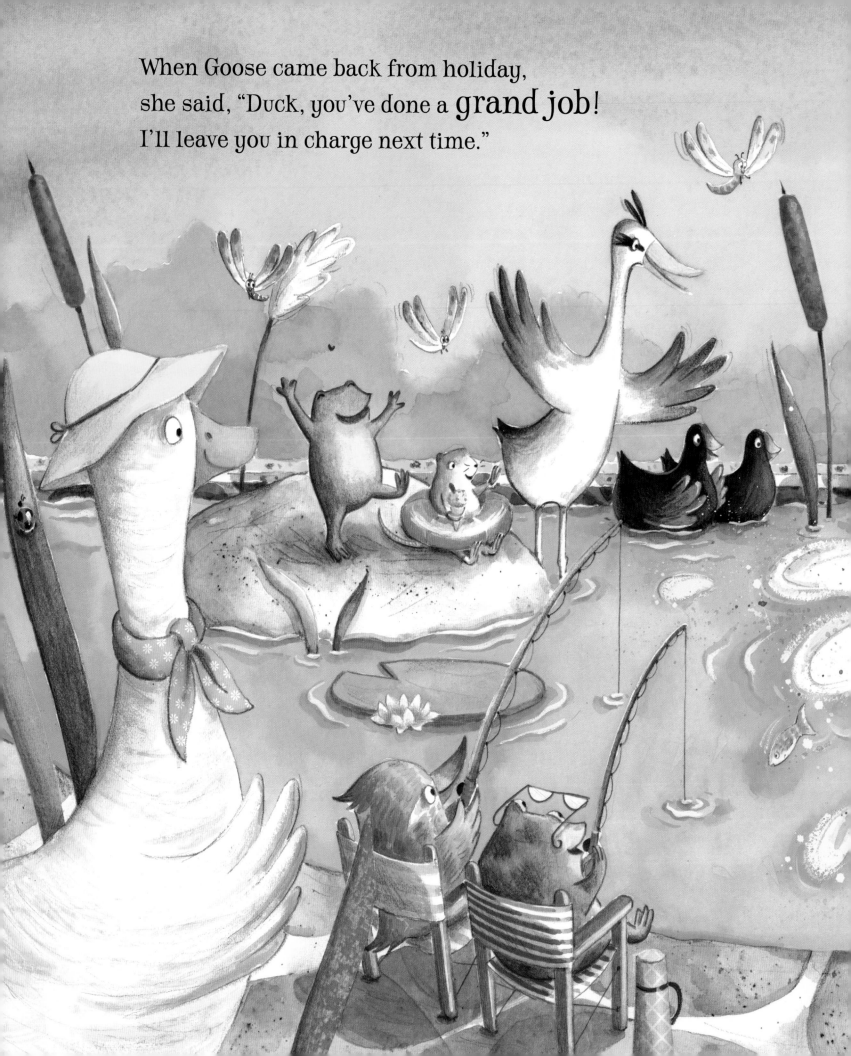

"No thank you, Goose." Duck laughed. "Being in charge is much too hard!"

And from that day on, Goose's pond was the **happiest** pond in the world, and Duck never said another bossy word.